YOUR MANY FACES

YOUR MANY FACES

Virginia Satir

Celestial Arts
Millbrae, California

Celestial Arts
231 Adrian Road
Millbrae, California 94030

First Printing, June 1978

Made in the United States of America

Cover Design: Abigail Johnston
Interior Illustrations: Patricia Edwards

Library of Congress Cataloging in Publication Data

Satir, Virginia M.
    Your many faces.

    1. Self-perception.   I. Title.
BF697.S26   158'.1   78-54477
ISBN 0-89087-187-6
ISBN 0-89087-120-5 pbk.

    2   3   4   5   6   7   —   84   83   82   81   80   79

*To all my friends, colleagues
and other people in the world,
who I know have marvelous
possibilities ahead of them.*

ACKNOWLEDGMENTS:

I wish to acknowledge and thank all those who gave of their time to read and respond to this effort in order to make this book clear and more readable, including Newell Weed, Wheelock Whitney, Lois James, Trae Boxer, Keith Berwick, Johanna Schwab, Jackie Schwartz, Anne Robertson, Lucille Hurwitz, Mary Jo Bulbrook, Ruth Turpin, Mary Harrell, Ruth Nicholls, Leonard and Merle Stine, Jane Levenberg Gerber, Yetta Bernhard, Vernon Sparks, Jane Donner, Vince Sweeney, Rachel Michaelsen, Shauna Adix, Ramona Adams, Sally Pierone, Fred Duhl and especially to John Levy, who, though startled to receive the manuscript, responded in his own inimitable way.

A special thanks to Hal Kramer, my publisher, for his constant encouragement to complete this project and to my editor, Joycelyn Moulton, for her patience and creativity.

CONTENTS

Introduction

Your Many Faces

*The Adventure of Discovering
the Miracle Within You*

I want to get you excited about *who you are, what
you are, what you have,* and *what can still be* for
you. I want to inspire you to see that you can go far
beyond where you are right now. This book is my
invitation to you to have a very special experience
with yourself, one that can open up all kinds of
new possibilities for you.

I can offer this invitation because you are a member
of the human race, and as such, *you are a miracle.*
Furthermore, you are a "one of a kind" miracle.
Let's consider the evidence. Each fingerprint on
every human being is different. Imagine, four bil-
lion people now present in the world, plus all those
who have come before and will come in the future.
All have their own unique fingerprints. There are
no duplicates. How could anyone think up so many
variations? That really boggles my mind. And yet,
it is an indisputable fact. Each of us is different.

It is also true that any surgeon who learns his or her surgery anywhere in the world can successfully operate on any human being, regardless of culture, race, nationality, language, age, occupation, religious affiliation, or political persuasion; because hearts, heads, and other parts of the anatomy will always be in relatively the same place. Correspondingly, children are always conceived in the same way and are birthed from the same place. We are also all the same.

Furthermore, consider the fantastic array of systems within the human body. Where else, in one small place, can you find a television; telephone; camera; radio; telegraph; computer; sewage, plumbing, heating and cooling systems; factories making all kinds of products: blood, chemicals, tissue, bones and sweat; all done up in one small unit, your body.

Take a moment to look around you and you will see that people come in all kinds of wrappings, all kinds of colors, speak in all kinds of languages and cook in a thousand different ways. People perform incredible feats including unbelievable destruction and repulsive cruelty, as well as unparalled generosity, sometimes sacrificing everything, including their lives, for the love and care of their fellow man. People, including myself, are my fascination, my source of nurture, delight, growth, struggle and pain. All of us share in the whole range of emotions, which I often call our *juices*, our feelings—anger, joy, fear, curiosity, love, excitement, helplessness and powerfulness. What triggers these feelings in each of us is different, but the capacity for these feelings is the same.

You have your own special wrapping, your own size, color, features, sex, age, background, experiences, thoughts, feelings and approaches to things, as do I. Yet at the same time each of us is a combination of *sameness* and *differentness* to every other human being. With some groups of people we may feel more alike, for example, women with women, men with men, or artists with artists. Oftentimes we tend to stay close to that which is familiar, and to turn away from that which is unfamiliar.

I want to challenge this idea. I think we have lost a lot of life's riches, and are continuing to do so, because we haven't learned the lesson of our own uniqueness. No matter how much alike we think we are, we are still different, and no matter how different we think we are, we are still alike. If you believe, as many people do, that your sameness creates your basis for trust and safety, and your differentness creates your problems, then you are using only half your resources. Everyone would like to be without problems and if you think that differentness creates your problems, you will use your energy to get rid of it. I think sameness can be comfortable but if that is all there is, in time it leads to boredom. Differentness can be a source of difficulty, but it also holds the key to a lot of locked up energy and experiences that make life exciting and fulfilling.

Allow yourself to think in terms of all your parts, the ones with which you are very familiar, the ones which have not been developed and the ones which you may not even know exist. Think of each of your parts as a resource, regardless of whether it is the same or different from anyone else's or whether you consider it good or bad. Whatever you have represents new possibilities of yourself. This book is about exploring these parts and learning how they can work for you to develop your possibilities. I am calling those different parts *YOUR MANY FACES.*

Virginia Satir

Lifting the Cover

If you were taught similar things to me, you probably grew up believing the world was simply divid-
ed into good and bad and right and wrong. And, if
you were to *lift the cover on yourself*, the chances
were good that you would have the horrible shock
of seeing all the bad and wrong things glaring up at
you in a worse state than you had ever imagined.
That is the naked truth many expect.

Some people think if they "lift the cover" there will
be all kinds of things reaching out demanding immediate satisfaction so they will feel suffocated and

torn by "things" pulling at them, increasing the burdens. The "things" I should have done but didn't; ought to do but can't. Some people think when they "lift the cover" it is going to be full of holes, dark recesses that will suck them into the abyss of the beyond and they will be lost forever. I've even heard some people say, they were afraid they'd find skills or abilities that they would never be able to fulfill. But some people don't want to "lift the cover" because "what I don't know doesn't hurt me," and besides, they are fine the way they are.

Some people don't "lift the cover" because they don't know there is a cover and don't know there is anything to them except what they see or hear or what other people tell them. Described this way it seems a little absurd, and yet these are frequent responses to lifting the cover, discovering the unknown about yourself. All the secrets, yearnings and fears of one's inner self often feel like a Pandora's Box which, once opened, may contaminate the universe, or certainly obliterate the owner.

In addition to these possibilities there are some yet unknown ones, some undeveloped buds, like mushrooms growing in the dark, that hold new possibilities. Once the barriers of negative expectation have been dealt with and we decide to take the risk to look, we can make some amazing discoveries.

We will begin our experience by visiting the Theater of the Inside where in the first act we will observe and get to know some of our parts, and the ways in which they behave. In the second act we will learn ways to deal with and use our parts, or faces, to discover new possibilities for ourselves. After the theater we will meet some famous faces from history, politics, entertainment and sports in order to compare and learn from *their* faces, the ones which they presented to the world and as a result, how they are remembered in history. In an amusement park we will visit a merry-go-round to look at our own faces from a different perspective. Finally, in an art gallery, we will observe the delightful balance of a mobile to learn about freedom and equilibrium in motion. All these experiences will help us to discover new possibilities for ourselves.

The Theater of the Inside

Act One

Lifting the Cover

Use your imagination and come with me to a very private place, deep within yourself, where each of us lives but few of us reveal what it's like to be there. It is our THEATER OF THE INSIDE which plays constantly, around the clock. You never know what is playing until you get there—tragedy, comedy, documentary, a morality play or a romantic love story. It might even be your own production of Little Orphan Annie, or quite possibly, the Old Woman in the Shoe.

Let's go into your mind which houses this theater. I'll join you. As we step inside we are handed the program for tonight.

THE THEATER OF THE INSIDE

boldly presents
tonight's play

YOUR MANY FACES

rated G

Act I   *Lifting the Cover*

intermission

Act II   *Who is in Charge?*

Your many faces are the players,
Everyone Welcome
Male and Female
Young and Old

Admission: Your attention and willing consideration of new
possibilities.

CAST OF CHARACTERS,
in order of their appearance

The "voice" of the outside—the "they" of society
Anger
Intelligence
Love
Stupidity
Power and friend
(Manipulation)
Helplessness
Hope
Jealousy
Humor
Sex

and their many relatives or variations,
too numerous to mention

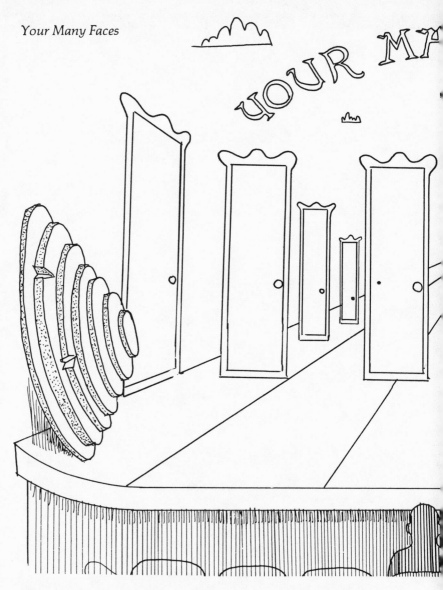

The theater is a giant circular space. We look up to see a domelike structure high above us. Probably this is where the spotlight will be. The stage is directly beneath the dome. As we enter there is only enough light to see more than just the bare outline of things. The light grows gradually

brighter and we begin to make out a series of doors all around the back of the stage which might be dressing rooms but right now there are no names on the doors. Although the stage is totally quiet we begin to notice other things.

To our right is a huge gadget that looks like a lighted football scoreboard with a giant thermometer. It has numbers which start with zero and go up to one hundred in bold, black type. There is a column going up filled with a luminescent blue-green fluid. Sticking out from one side of the thermometer gadget are two large spotlight looking objects, about midway up is a red light and at the top, a gold one. Neither is lighted. Under the gold light is a list of words headed "Energy Providers:" Hopefulness, Helpfulness, Powerfulness, New Possibilities, Change, and Choice. Under the red light is another list of words headed "Energy Depleters:" Hopelessness, Helplessness, Powerlessness, No Possibility, No Change, No Choice. Obviously, there must be a connection between the energy providers, the gold light, and the energy depleters, the red light. Above, in the boldest letters of all, are the words: "Energy, Your Source of Life."

Apparently this thermometer registers feelings. It makes me think that our feelings must be capable of both depleting and providing energy. The red and gold lights are probably signals to indicate which is doing what. That seems important. Does it mean there is a way we can experience things differently? Does it mean if we know more about our feelings we can change some very fundamental things about our lives? Could it possibly mean that we really aren't stuck with the way things are right now? That is a very hopeful and encouraging thought.

ENERGY, YOUR SOURCE OF LIFE

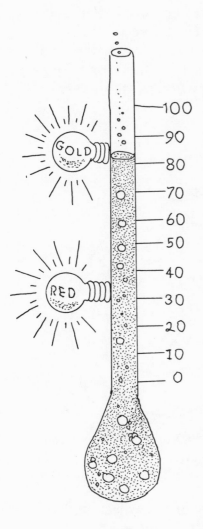

ENERGY PROVIDERS
Hopefulness
Helpfulness
Powerfulness
New Possibilities
Change
Choice

ENERGY DEPLETERS
Hopelessness
Helplessness
Powerlessness
No Possibility
No Change
No Choice

On the other side of the stage, to our left, my attention is drawn to another device, equally as large as the thermometer gadget and directly across from it. It has rings of color—eight to be exact— and over the top are the words "Universal Resource Wheel." It, too, is unlighted but it is covered with dust and cobwebs as though it hasn't been used for a long time. Somehow I know this wheel holds another of the keys for hope.

UNIVERSAL RESOURCE WHEEL

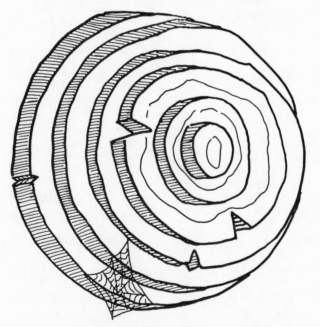

My eyes move to the right of the wheel and my stomach tightens into a painful knot as I read a list of things called: Rules for Being a Good Person.

There are no cobwebs or dust on this one. It is brightly lighted and looks to be in daily use. It reads, "I Must Always Be: Right, Clean, Bright, Sane, Good, Obedient, Healthy, No matter what the cost or situation, for, Everyone counts more than I, and, Who am I to ask for anything for myself?"

RULES FOR BEING A GOOD PERSON
I MUST ALWAYS BE:
Right
Clean
Bright
Sane
Good
Obedient
Healthy

NO MATTER WHAT THE COST
OR SITUATION
for
Everyone counts more than I
and
Who am I to ask for anything for myself?

It seems that throughout my entire life I have run into this in some form or another, and almost everywhere. I recognize it as the Universal Should List. I spent many years trying to make it work, but the best I could do was to succeed only some of the time. When I couldn't make it work I felt very bad about myself.

The more I look around the more I see, which is, of course, natural. The important thing is to get yourself to look. Across from the Universal Should List, just to the right of the thermometer-scoreboard gadget, I notice another large sign. At the top in big glistening letters are written the words: "I—Me—Myself." Underneath in very clear though not as large letters appear the words: "I can be: whole, joyful, loving, healthy, intelligent, sexual, creative, humorous, competent." In less bold letters, under that I can barely make out the words: "It is all possible."

I   ME   MYSELF
I can be
Whole
Joyful
Loving
Healthy
Intelligent
Sexual
Creative
Humorous
Competent
"It is all possible."

I remember the many times I have doubted those words. Like many other people I thought that was only for those who have degrees, make a lot of money, or have the right parents and good oppor-tunities. But not for me. Again, the muscles in my stomach tighten. The light is getting fuller now. High in the dome above me I see clearly written *Your Many Faces,* as if to leave no doubt, in case we had not read the program, of what the play is to be.

Suddenly I am aware of music and realize it has been playing in many variations, soft, loud, slow, fast, heavy, light, on key and out of key ever since we arrived. It is as though it is following the full repertoire of life's moods, struggles and joys, as they shift and change. The music fades slightly and the names on the doors light up. They are Anger, Intelligence, Love, Stupidity, Power and friend (Manipulation), Helplessness, Jealousy and Sex. From offstage a strong, menacing "voice" opens the scene.

"Do you always have to mess everything up!"

In response, a figure, obviously Anger, wearing a cast iron suit with large spikes sticking out of it, storms on stage bellowing, "Who do you think you are! Who are you to talk!" pointing a bony finger in the direction of the voice. Anger's neck is bright red and its face looks mean. I am frightened.

Now the door of Intelligence swings open and a figure with a very large head strides out, apparently curious to see what is going on. "Now, now," Intelligence says confidently, "let's bring some reason to this situation, let's analyze it and see what's going on here."

Anger whirls around to face Intelligence. I know there is going to be violence. Turning contemptuous, Anger shakes a clenched fist at Intelligence. "Talk, talk, talk, all you do is talk. Reason! Bah!"

To the right of the stage the red light is on full and the energy level is running up and down as though it is being chased. At this point Love bounds through the door resplendent in a flowing robe and dramatically announces "Love conquers all!" quickly wrapping Anger captive in its arms.

Anger is obviously shocked and insulted and re-
wards Love with a sharp pinch. Within moments,
mayhem, chaos and confusion erupt. Love screams
and quickly retreats with a look of devastation and
a cry of despair.

Love's quick action has served some purpose
though because the left side of Anger's iron suit

29

falls off. Anger is too angry to notice, and shouts accusingly "Love is for weaklings! Only weaklings cry!" Intelligence is getting nervous; apparently it is trying to think of something reasonable to say, but is unsuccessful.

Meanwhile, Stupidity shuffles in, looking very much like how Intelligence feels. Stupidity is quite a sight, dressed in clothes several sizes too tight, full of holes, making unintelligible sounds and drooling. It is pathetic. I wonder whether this character is trying to be funny or is in real agony.

Stupidity is too much for Anger; the rest of its suit of armor falls off. Anger is very vulnerable now but seems totally unaware of it. Stupidity has stopped the action and is dominating the scene. Anger, upstaged, begins to shrivel and moan almost as unintelligibly as Stupidity. What a group of characters. Love is wailing in the corner, Intelligence is dumb. The gauge is red and the energy has dropped to between helplessness and hopelessness. The condition is close to paralysis and something has to be done or it will be too late.

At this point, two very imposing figures approach. They are Power and Manipulation, who share a dressing room, and as usual, are all wrapped up in each other. Power looks confident but there is a

piercing gleam in its eye. Its body is lean and it looks somewhat like a robot, fully equipped with automatic buttons. We are too far away to read what the buttons say but it must be something like, "If you can't make it happen any other way, force it."

Manipulation is a funny-looking little person with one arm in front and one behind, and a head that turns all the way around. Its legs manipulate so sometimes one leg and one hand are in front and sometimes behind. It is truly an all-purpose character. Clearly, whatever happens, Manipulation will have some way to deal with it.

In a cold voice Power says, "Anger must be stamped out. Anger is dangerous." With a sweet smile on its face, Manipulation approaches Anger as if to be a friend. When Anger drops its guard, Manipulation and Power, working as a team, one on either side, begin to pull Anger apart. Right or wrong at least someone is trying to do something.

Love utters a shrill cry of fright and pleads, "Don't hurt, don't hurt!" The energy is high but it is being used dangerously. I can feel the terror. What can come of this? At exactly that moment, from outside somewhere, the "voice" thunders, "STOP IT RIGHT NOW! GOOD PEOPLE DON'T BEHAVE LIKE THIS! THEY DON'T EVEN FEEL LIKE THIS! STOP! IMMEDIATELY!"

All action on stage ceases and from the corner of my eye I see the energy in the thermometer plunge. The figures slink back to their dressing rooms. Immediately the names on the doors change to: Banished, Ignored, Rejected, Paralyzed, Punished and Unclaimed. A terrible feeling of powerlessness, hopelessness, and helplessness fills the room. The outer problem is solved, at least for the time being. Despite this, all of us know the inner struggle remains, though for the moment, it is out of sight.

How many times had I lived through this very scene, stifling my feelings to please the outside world. Even the thought of it makes me feel sick inside. My further thoughts were lost in the din of wailing and knocking, moans, ludicrous laughter and buzzing sounds coming from behind the doors.

It was a relief to hear the "voice" apparently feeling guilty, call out, "Well, if you are so helpless we will just have to deal with it. If you were more mature, this sort of thing wouldn't happen all the time."

With much weeping and wailing, Helplessness creeps out, pleading and promising to be good if only nobody would fight anymore. I almost cried out, "Stop it, shut up, I can't stand it!" I was remembering the Universal Should, "No matter what is going on, no matter what it costs, look happy and be nice!"

Helplessness is frantically begging for the right to live. This must have sounded like a distress signal

to Power who strides back into the room immediately, exuding authority. Power looks neither
friendly nor frightening but appears totally objec-
tive. However, for Helplessness, just the sight of
Power brings on another flood of helplessness. Although Power had always seemed desirable to
Helplessness, there never seemed to be a way to in-
troduce it. Helplessness knows, deep inside, that it
must find a way because without Power, it is
doomed. But once again, Helplessness finds itself
cowering in the corner.

For a moment Power looks shocked and then
frightened. It had no desire to hurt anyone, only a
wish to bring about some relevant action, to let

them know it isn't necessary to spend the rest of life futilely weeping and wailing. This time Power is carrying a small do-it-yourself kit, on the side of which is a sign, FOR THE MAINTENANCE AND REPAIR OF MIRACLES. Power explains, "If you are willing to take the risk to meet me, you will learn how to comfort your own Helplessness, but first you have to learn not to be afraid of me, your Power."

I feel a little better. The thermometer has risen to Hopefulness and for the first time the gold light is on. Love is peeking out from behind the door, obviously wanting to try again. It must have learned a lesson before because this time its entrance is a bit more cautious, and certainly more timely. Love reaches out to Power but this time waits for its response. Power gently takes Love's outstretched hand. With Love and Power linked, Helplessness is willing to take the risk of expressing honestly what it wants. Thus, supported by the comfort of Love and the support of Power, Helplessness turns into Courage. The energy gauge rises to a level between Change and New Possibilities and the gold light is shining brightly. For several minutes there is peace and it seems as though the inner problem has been resolved.

Suddenly, there is a crash and our old friend, Manipulation, stomps forward, legs, head and hands rotating in all directions. It sounds like the voice of doom, "This won't last, you know. You've got to be tough in this world—take your lumps and quit your moaning. After all, it's a hard world out there. Never mind what *you* want. You had better do what *other people* want. *That* is where your security lies." Manipulation is persuasive enough to make Love, Power and Courage stop and bow their heads. It was true, you do have to think twice before you take on the world out there.

Could Love do something about this? Could Helplessness, now turned to Courage, help? Power seems to be considering something. After all, to some people, Love does mean weakness and to some, Helplessness feels contemptible, Courage is fleeting and Power can be dangerous. Believing that, the best way may be to make a deal with the "outside." You can live that way; thousands of people do. Of course, you may not get what you want, you may have lots of headaches, and your stomach may hurt, but then, life is a grim business anyway. It is like giving up. A pall of resignation and quiet paralysis comes over the room. It begins to rain outside. The gauge quickly drops again to hopelessness and then to powerlessness. The red light is on now. The moment for an important decision is at hand.

As though struck by a bolt of lightning the door to Intelligence flies open. Intelligence, now with a smaller head, more in proportion to the rest of its body, quietly walks forward and in a soft but clear voice says, "Yes, the demands of others are important but so are yours. We must find creative ways to consider both. One thing stands out above all else; each one of us must feel centered and must feel like a whole, valuable person before we can do justice to others or to ourselves."

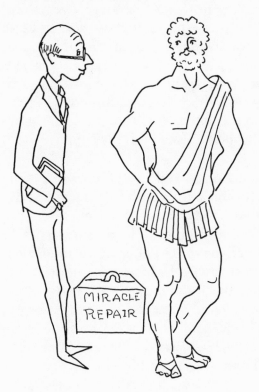

What a novel idea! How delightful to have a little Intelligence around. (Everybody's got some, although they don't always act as though they do.) Power perks up a little, remembering there are other possibilities in its Repair Kit. Suddenly a bright expression comes over Power's face and it says, "I'll take that risk. I think it's worth a try to do what needs to be done for ourselves."

Helplessness, who had lost some of its courage, is remembering how big and tough everything on the outside is and especially how you have to be so careful not to make people mad. Helplessness begins to plead with Power, saying, "Don't do anything hasty, or we might all get hurt! Let's not make things worse than they are already. We can probably live through it." (I thought, how many times have I trapped myself with that one.)

Love seems unmoved by the plea of Helplessness. Instead it joins hands with Intelligence and together with Power they stand three abreast, supporting each other and giving Helplessness comfort, saying, "You'll have to allow us to take over now." That didn't make Helplessness understand things any better but it did make it feel better. In fact, not only does Helplessness feel relieved, it begins to feel hope. The gold light starts to flicker on as the gauge moves steadily toward Change. Somehow in the face of Love, Power and Intelligence, Manipulation undergoes a change and offers to become a Manager! As a good Manager it asks the people involved what they need instead of deciding what's good for them without asking.

The thermometer is nearing ninety and the gold light is brilliant. All seems quiet in a new way.

There is a vitality and a feeling of trust in the room. It is a wonderful feeling.

Suddenly I am caught off guard. There is a terrible clamor as though the roof caved in. Jealousy charges in with all the fires of passion and roars in a scornful voice, "How *dare* you feel like this. How *dare* you feel good when there are so many others who feel miserable!" I feel as though I've been stabbed.

Helplessness starts to wail again, 'I knew it, I knew it wouldn't last. We'll all be punished." Of course, Helplessness has now turned to Pessimist. Anger becomes sarcastic, "Pain and trouble are to be expected, they are normal." Sounding like the voice of authority, it continues, "I suppose you think you can be different? That's a good one! Only children believe in fairy tales." And now, becoming Blame, Anger raves on, "You want to make all those folks feel jealous and make them think you are better than they are? Shame on you!"

The gold light flickers out. A cold silence, like a
wind from the Arctic fills the room. The gauge
drops to the Energy Depletors settling on Hopelessness, a close relative to Despair.

A funny, erratic
substance begins
to float in from
another room.
It is Humor, acting
like a   fool.
"Let's not take all
this seriously.
Who cares about
anything anyway,"
it says, laughing
raucously and
hanging from the
ceiling. "You're just
making all this up.
Nobody feels anything,
everything is a tin cup!"

Humor's effort
to change things is only
making them more tragic.
Humor has many faces too,
not all of them funny. Shame is spreading throughout the room. In fact, the whole situation is shame-
ful. The gauge is not even registering.

Now, out of nowhere, comes Sex. How shocking! How could Sex enter at a time like this? It probably thought it was its duty. I know the irreverence of Sex at a time like this but I also know how many times Sex is used to try to change such a situation.

There is a feeling of desperation; Shame sits on the doorstep, Helplessness is wailing, Power is out to lunch and Love goes off to its room. Guilt dominates the scene. Once more, there is paralysis. The gauge remains motionless.

From the outside world, in a loud monotone, the "voice" commands, "GET TO WORK. RIGHT NOW. FORGET ALL ABOUT THIS FEELING NONSENSE. WORK IS WHAT COUNTS." Actually, this is a relief and for fifteen minutes everybody works hard and nobody talks. Again it looks like the outer problem has been solved. The gauge is still frozen, neither light is on. But now fatigue is setting in. Silently, one by one, each figure steals back to its place behind the doors marked Banished, Ignored, Rejected, Paralyzed, Punished and Unclaimed.

I become aware that this is the state of quiet desperation when nothing really bad or really good happens. Life just goes on, day after day. You are out of the overt conflict and left with a ceaseless yearning for something better, but there is no energy available to act on it.

Intermission

The first act is over and there is time to think about what we have seen. Much of it was disturbing, and I have to remind myself that there were some hopeful scenes as well as bad ones. I don't think I understood everything, but I definitely felt it all. One thing I was clear about, we are always in constant motion. We are reacting and responding to the inside and the outside all the time.

People don't feel this way because they are ornery, or because they want to make trouble for themselves or others. They really want to be good people, to bury the bad things, to keep their lives tolerable by not having so many demands. They don't want to fool around with things they don't know about, or be obligated to develop everything they have. They want to try to give their lives some sense of ease. These are their intentions and it all sounds very reasonable. However, my experience over these last many years has been that as life goes on for many people it becomes draining, boring and not very pleasant. In effect, we live in an emotional jail without knowing it.

Breaking Out of Your Emotional Jail

Most of us live in an emotional jail because we want to be good. We surround ourselves with a whole network of "shoulds" that are often in conflict with our wishes and our abilities. (Remember the Universal Should List?) This almost always results in a sense of failure, needless frustration and disappointment.

I am quite aware we cannot control the weather or many of the things outside of ourselves, but we can learn new ways to cope with those things we can't control. Everyone is familiar with the various ways in which different people cope with the same event. The event does not dictate the way of coping. The integration (your harmonious use of your parts) of the event into your life determines how you cope.

This network of "shoulds" includes a lot of internal dialogue about whether or not "they" would approve. The "they" can be anybody, your mother, your father, your boss, your Aunt Minnie, the ones you look to to decide whether what you are doing is or is not okay. (The "voice" from the play.) Where would we be if all the inventors and all the people who have risked new directions, and often made great discoveries, had waited for somebody to say it was okay before they tried it?

All too often, people are unaware that through their lack of knowledge, imagination and awareness, they have built high walls around themselves over which they cannot see their possibilities. Fortunately for us these walls that look like cement derive their strength only from our thoughts. There is a difference between a concrete wall outside of us and the walls we erect in our minds. Dealing effectively with the wall outside is related to the wall we have inside. If we feel trapped inside, little creative energy will be available to cope creatively. Our inside jailers represent that which we regard as threatening. The guards are our fears, ever present, who see to it that we stay where we are. As long as we are afraid, we can't move. These jailers and guards, of course, are our own concoctions, mostly derived from threats of authority figures in our past, and which we brought to our present without any critical evaluation of their usefulness. The guards represent our worries about not being loved or valued. There is, therefore, no opportunity in that jail to test out new possibilities. The beginning of the breaking out of your emotional jail simply starts with a new thought, "There must be something more, and I will take the risk to take a look." That leads to hope which becomes a new possibility.

We are always trying to get out of our emotional jail. It is so uncomfortable so much of the time. Mostly we try by begging, threatening, or pleasing other people, trying to get them to do it for us. This makes sense if we believe our jailers are only on the outside. One can get some temporary success from this, here and there, but in general these efforts end in failure with massive feelings of helplessness, rage and guilt.

Suppose instead we were to accept the fact that our biggest jailers are inside; that we begin by taking the risk of making a study of how our thoughts, feelings, body and soul all work together. All of us have beliefs that, when held up to the light of investigation, turn out to be almost ridiculous; yet we have lived without questioning them. Your study will doubtlessly reveal beliefs of this kind that you will challenge once you find them.

Once having let go of old beliefs which are no longer applicable to your life, you are going into unknown territory for which there is no map. You make it as you go along. This is what risk is all about. Like everyone who forges trails in the wilderness, you can make many starts. One place might look promising until you get there. Once there, you may find that it didn't fulfill its promise and you have to take a new direction. However, you might just as easily find that it delivered more than its promise and that many new doors are opened to you as a result. This is all part of discovery. There is no certain route that you can map out ahead of time. You only know where you have been after you have been there.

Many people lose their battles on the outside because they waste their energy on the inside. Our inner life and our outer coping are linked. One feeds into the other. As children most of us were taught how to conform and to be obedient. Until we learned otherwise that was all we knew. Whatever pain we had to endure to continue life, we took inside, believing that was how life was and thus began building the walls of our emotional jail.

It is a giant step to take the risk of beginning to question these old learnings. It puts us into the scary unknown. The struggle is difficult and the way often unclear. However, once having become explorers in the service of ourselves, we break out of jail and continued growth is possible. Our energy can now be used to find and explore new possibilities, rather than to continue to waste energy defending our old beliefs in an effort to make life bearable.

The sad part for me is to know that many people are living in an emotional jail without recognizing it. They know only that they are vaguely unhappy and depressed, waiting for some magic time when things will be different but which never seems to come. They have sentenced themselves to this fate for failing to live up to the Universal Should List, which they ignorantly accepted as the way to live the good life. NOBODY CAN LIVE UP TO THIS LIST. It is the door to an emotional jail. In that jail there is nothing to do but live out the sentence. It is only when we can get out that we have a chance for a new life. Lifting the Cover, the first act of Your Many Faces, is one dramatization that goes on inside ourselves when we are in that jail. Many of us have not yet gone beyond the first act.

The second act is about to begin: The play is still YOUR MANY FACES and the second act is called "Who Is In Charge?"

Act Two

Who Is In Charge?

This time, as we enter, the theater is well lighted and everything is easily seen. Facing us is an attractive human figure, wearing a white robe, appearing neither male nor female, and could be either. A wide azure blue belt with the word MIRACLE embroidered in sparkling thread encircles the waist. A headband with the word OWNER in large illuminated letters is worn with pride. The feet of the figure are well grounded, the arms reach toward the sky and the body is free to move, taking in all that is around. The face is appealingly textured from life's experiences. I sense that this person will welcome whatever life brings and be willing to sort, channel and challenge it in terms of its usefulness at the moment. This person will see the outside as an important part of life but will know the degree of involvement with the outside world is only as rich and effective as the degree of wholeness and freedom inside.

The labels on the doors are still as they were at the end of the first act, Banished, Ignored, Rejected, Paralyzed, Punished, and Unclaimed. There are loud, unpleasant sounds emanating from the rooms that are scary. There is excitement and a little tension as the human figure observes the names on the doors. I hear it say, "I'm going to find out what's behind that door." I can see that it is gathering courage to take this step. Finally, ready to face this unknown, the figure steps in the direction of the door marked Punished, pauses a moment before knocking, almost as if to say, "Am I really willing to see what's there."

There is determination in the voice as it says, "I am scared, but I will never find out what's there until I look." With that the figure opens the door. After all, it is the owner and has the only key.

What it sees is an ugly face. It is our old friend, Anger, Blame/Sarcasm. The owner says, "Just a moment," and goes to the door where Love lives. What Anger, Blame/Sarcasm needs is some Love, because its owner has seen behind the outer face, and recognized that terrible feeling of being unloved. Helplessness, which is still wailing next

door, is a very close relative to Anger. On the way to asking Love to appear, it occurs to the owner that Intelligence would be helpful, and stopping at its door, invites it to come. Then the owner remembers that although Love might make Anger feel better and Intelligence would understand what was happening, both would be useless without the presence of Power. The owner knows that Power can be used in many ways, but is confident that it can be controlled.

The owner brings out its imprisoned Power, links arms with Love and Intelligence and proceeds to the yowling Anger. By this time Helplessness is crouched halfway under Anger's bed, apparently fearful of being beaten. Anger has one foot on Helplessness. It is as though Anger is trying to punish its own feelings of Helplessness. This is a new problem.

The owner takes charge of this by announcing. "Yes, you are all faces of me, you are mine. I am in charge of managing you. You are my Love, my Intelligence and my Power. I also own you, my Helplessness and my Anger. Now you, my Anger, are giving me a clear message that I have been neglecting something. You feel threatened and fearful. What have I done to you?"

An interesting thing happens then. Anger takes its foot off Helplessness, Helplessness begins to look less frightened, and Anger, of all people, starts to sob. "I *have* been neglected, and you wouldn't pay any attention to me. You were furious with your daughter the other day and you knew I was there, but you acted as though I didn't even exist. When I gave you a headache you took an aspirin so you couldn't feel it."

A look of awareness comes upon the owner's face. "That's true," it acknowledges, "I didn't have the courage to tell my daughter how I really felt, because I was afraid she would turn away from me and then I would have to deal with it. Actually I was enraged inside but I tried to cover you up. It was right for you to make all that noise. Sometimes I am quite deaf. I know now that it wouldn't have been so terrible to have told her that I felt angry. She must have known that she was being inconsiderate but I often worry that I will hurt people if I tell them I am angry. Now I know that I only cut down my energy and deprive them of the truth by hiding it."

Anger is beginning to feel satisfied and Power puts its arm around Anger's shoulder. It becomes clear that the problem is not having an angry face, it is the terrible hurt that comes when it is suppressed. To ask Love to soothe Anger without first recognizing the problem is too great a step. (Anger noticed is the first step toward new possibilities.)

When the first confrontation was made, energy was again running wildly up and down the scale and the red light was flashing. After the confrontation was made and accepted, the energy went up to a hundred and the gold light was flashing. Everything was going well.

Then, as in life, another challenge appears. Manipulation enters uninvited and blithely accuses, "I guess you know your mother would never approve of this!" Whereupon Intelligence steps forward and says, "I agree with you. My mother had different attitudes than I do. She might find it puzzling, or she might get worried. You see, she always thought that Anger was bad and could only make trouble. She thought the only intelligent approach was to keep it contained."

Manipulation is disarmed. It had expected an argument. This is a completely new idea and it requires some thought. Then Manipulation surprises even itself by offering its services as facilitator. Love gets a little worried at this very unusual switch and says, "Are you sure your mother will still love you if she knows you not only

57

feel angry but *show* it?" Whereupon the owner answers, "Maybe not right at the moment, because it will be such a surprise, but if I give her time she will know I do not do it out of hate for her but only wholeness for me." The energy which once again had been out of control stabilizes at New Possibilities when the owner takes charge. The gold light is on.

There is a quiet dignity in the room now and Humor, who had appeared like a fool before, enters wearing another face. "Isn't it funny," it says, "how absurd we really can be, to think that because we share feelings, it is certain we will stop being loved or great harm will come to us." This was indeed the birth of wisdom.

Jealousy, being hard to convince, isn't quite finished yet. "How can you feel *good*, when other people feel *bad?*"

Intelligence answers, "You see, it's like this. You can share without blaming. I have learned that my feeling good has nothing to do with anyone else feeling good or bad. I just misunderstood some things when I was growing up. I thought that if my mother smiled it was because I was good, and if she frowned it was because I was bad. It was like my mother couldn't be smiling or frowning about anything but me. Like I was in charge of her feelings. That, of course, is nonsense. My mother could smile or frown for lots of reasons besides me. Look at it this way. If I think I am so powerful that if I am feeling good, everybody else will have to feel bad, or even that I can make everybody else feel good if I'm feeling good, then I'm really insulting everybody, because I am acting as though they have no will or possibilities of their own. I don't want to insult people anymore. I want to give them my truth, my honesty, and my feelings and expect them to treat me as I am prepared to treat them. If I do this I will not be hiding from myself or blaming others, both of which are big energy drains. Instead I will be freeing and increasing my own energy and offering others something better."

While Intelligence is talking, Curiosity has been running around peeking between everyone's legs trying to see what is going on. Now it comes out with a very straight question. "You mean that everything can be perfect all the time! I had a terrible time when everyone was upset. That was an awful experience. I am certainly glad everything is so marvelous now. Do you suppose it will stay like this forever?"

With knowing smiles Intelligence, Power and Love explain patiently "No, there *is* no perfect way, and it *won't* stay this way forever. Getting into jams now and then is a part of life. The important thing is not to avoid jams but to know what to do when they happen and things seem dark and we feel paralyzed. We can change this situation by putting what we are feeling into words, by accepting and owning what we are feeling. Instead of trying to cover it up when we feel angry on the inside, we can simply say, "I am angry." We can say 'I feel' instead of 'You make me feel.' Have you noticed there is someone new in this room?"

Everyone looks around and there, a little figure dressed in green, with a pointed hat and light dancing feet, quickly makes his way to the center carrying a big sign, "I am the New Possibilities." In a pleasant voice it says, "I can only come out when things are clear, free and understood, and when people are willing to take new risks." At this moment, all of the parts are standing in a circle around the human figure. They are offering themselves to their owner with all of their variations from Helplessness to Helpfulness, from Hopelessness to

Hopefulness, from Powerlessness to Powerfulness, from Anger, Blame/Sarcasm to Joy. They are ready to help the owner to understand, to challenge, to grow, and to love. The owner acknowledges them saying, "You are all mine. Sometimes you overwhelm me and sometimes I forget some of you but I appreciate you. I am grateful when you call your presence to my attention in whatever state you happen to be in. Once I notice you I can begin to take charge of myself."

The gauge is now registering one hundred, the gold light is fully burning. Once in awhile the red light flashes on momentarily adding the right touch of color to the whole scene. It is a happy ending.

What Have We Learned?

For one thing that you probably have many parts that you have not yet discovered. All of these parts, whether you have owned them or not, are present in you. Becoming aware of them enables you to take charge of them, rather than be enslaved by them. Each of your parts is a vital source of energy. Each has many uses, and can harmonize with many other parts in ways to add even more energy.

Having many faces is an ordinary, everyday experience for everyone. When you go from sleep to waking each morning, your body goes through a process. You probably look disoriented and very far away. That could be your *distant face.* You are having a beautiful moment of loving and you probably show your *loving face.* You come across something that you don't understand and you will show your *puzzled face.* You feel good after a delicious meal and you show your *satisfied face.* Something has gone wrong, and you feel hurt or threatened, and then you might show your *angry face.* You have done something which you feel foolish about and you might show your *stupid face.* These faces are all part of almost every person's life.

Many people make an internal scoreboard and judge each face as being either good or bad. Would it sound very bizarre to entertain the idea that each of your faces, no matter how you have judged them in the past, can be used to work for you? They all contain vital energy. Most of us have worn a tired face from time to time. Tiredness is a condition in which your body is using all of its energy to maintain itself so there is none left over to sparkle on the outside. This is what was going on in Act One of our play.

Make a list for yourself, of all the different faces that you know about, dividing them into those which you label good and those you label bad. Each of your faces, regardless of whether you label it good or bad, holds the seed, the germ, so to speak, of new energy and new uses, something like finding a pretty face under a lot of dirt. I recommend just washing off the dirt and being careful not to destroy the whole face.

In Columbus' time, the world was believed to be flat, and all the other beliefs of that time reinforced the idea. Today if anyone were to seriously suggest the world was flat, no one would give it a second thought, not even as a possibility. The reason is because we have learned so much since that time and that old idea no longer fits in light of that new knowledge.

The same thing is true of human beings. We have, for a long time, felt that as human beings we were limited. We categorized, labeled, and measured ourselves and then made a niche to match. The niche became our boundary, so that our aim became filling niches instead of fulfilling our lives. We are becoming increasingly aware that we have limited ourselves by our thoughts and beliefs. They are much more powerful in shaping our lives than anything we are born with. It turns out when we learn to appreciate life in ourselves we have a greater appreciation of life in others, and this leads us closer to what we want, namely, closeness to others. It is hard to appreciate either ourselves or others when we are so busy making judgments.

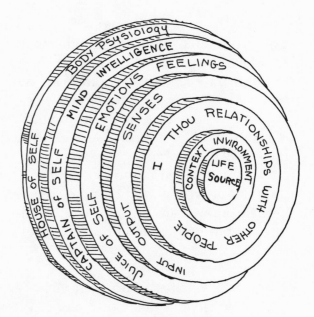

Your Resource Wheel

In our play at the Theater of the Inside, we saw a Resource Wheel. Let's get it out, brush the dust and cobwebs off and take a closer look at it. On the first layer in the center is that which you call yourself, your "I." Around your "I" is a body which is essentially your house. Around your body is your mind (brain) which we could call the captain of your ship. That is the part which analyzes what you see and hear. Around this layer are your emotions; I call them your "juice,"—pain, joy, anger, confusion—those parts of yourself which give you your feeling.

The next layer is concerned with your senses, your eyes, your ears, your nose, your mouth, the pores of your skin, all of which are the "holes" in which input from the outside comes in, and messages from your inside go out. If you were to bind up your eyes, your ears, your nose, your mouth, and all your skin, of course you would be dead right away. Let's suppose, however, you leave just enough uncovered so you can get air. Even then, pretty soon you would become completely disoriented from everything. You would still technically be alive but you would for all practical purposes be dead.

The next layer has to do with your I—thou part. We cannot live in this world alone. We can't even come into this world without the help of two other people. Relating to other people is a fact of life. How we do this influences our health, our feelings about ourselves and our uses of ourselves. In short, this is our communication layer.

Around all this we have a soul, which regardless of what name we call it, is really a life force. This is my view, which may or may not have a connection with organized religion. Anybody can go to the drugstore and buy all the chemical ingredients present in a human being. With inflated prices it probably would cost $3.49. But no one to date has been able to take those ingredients and make a human being. The soul is that life essence in each of us, our central source.

All of this occurs within a context, the next layer, which is made up of time, space, light, air, water, sound, color, weather and seasons. Extended to its farthest realms all of the layers become the Universe. Each of us is part of this Universe and being so gives us our Miracle status. All layers are present, and not only does each layer have life, but the layers are interacting; our thoughts act on our feelings, our feelings act on our thoughts, our thoughts and feelings act on our bodies, our bodies and our senses act on our thoughts and feelings, and so forth. There is a whole interacting, continually moving, dynamic link between and among parts going on inside of us at every moment. Discovering the way these parts interact lets us know how we are treating ourselves and, incidentally, others.

Our intention is not to make you a scholar of each of your parts, but instead to invite you to discover, own, and learn about the various layers and how they interact in you. Each serves a different function for you. Each has the capacity to stand temporarily by itself, but only temporarily. Each part needs the others to function fully.

It's fun to make up your own wheel and for each one of the rings, layers or parts choose a color that you feel fits it. Make a ring of that color. Put them all together and you have your own personal Resource Wheel. To use myself as an example, I like to leave the center "I" white. For me, "body" is a beautiful water blue; when I think "mind" it is a rich pearl gray; when I think "feelings" it is a soft rose; for "senses" it is bright green; for my "interaction with others" it is a rosy beige. When I think of my "soul" I think of bright gold. The "context" for me is a soft dark green and the "planetary" is a vivid purple. Your colors will probably be different. Perhaps this will do nothing more than alert you to the fact that not only do we have many parts, but they all have a different feeling to you.

If you happen to be one of those persons who associates rhythm or tones to colors, you could go to a musical instrument and pick out the tone that each of these colors signifies and develop your own symphony. To carry my prose a little further, I think of the area in the middle of your body as being a bright sun (your "I" in the Resource Wheel) that casts its rays all over your body and fans out into the space around you and beyond, through all the layers. Each ray covers the color spectrum. Perhaps even now, just reading this, you are feeling an expanded sense of yourself. The sun never really sets, it only appears that way, because we are not in a position to see it. Sometimes we may not feel the sunshine, only the night, but the sun will be there in the morning, as surely as the earth turns. That is faith. Faith in the existence of that which is, even though it is not always visible. The night features the moon and stars so the spectrum becomes muted by the night but sparkles silver from the moon. Expect the gold colors when the sun is on your side and the silver when the moon is out, and enjoy each for what it is, not asking the moon to give you what the sun has, and vice versa. With this kind of thinking the Universal Shoulds become Helpful Guides, When and If They Fit. Finding out how we think about what we see and hear, what we feel, what we say, how we look and sound is the place to start the discovery of who and what we are. How we relate to all our layers has probably as many variations and possibilities as our fingerprints.

In our Theater of the Inside we saw two variations, or possibilities, of an internal drama taking place. At the closing of the play, what seems to stand out is that things change. Something very important happened in that last act. Things changed and we saw some new possibilities which hopefully can add some new dimensions to our lives. When we really take charge of ourselves we have the power to cope differently and we can make our own map for our lives. That is our hope. That is our life process, and that is our opportunity.

Looking with New Eyes—
Taking New Risks

New thoughts and beliefs are the main source for opening up new possibilities. Our willingness to risk exploring these possibilities through action is the next step. There is a secure feeling about staying with what we already know, and a scariness about venturing out into areas unfamiliar to us. To go where we have not been, either literally or figuratively, usually has two parts, excitement and scariness, both of which involve the adrenal glands and come from the same root.

Fritz Perls used to say, "In scariness or anxiety, breathe a little and you will feel the excitement. Hold your breath and you'll get scared again." What I am suggesting is that the step into a new place, either a new idea, a new physical space, or a new direction, carries with it the process of excitement and scare, and catapults us into the change process. One thing that will always help to balance you is to consciously breathe; that way you have positive proof that you are still living. Many people are so bogged down with catastrophic expectations about what will happen that they do not venture out.

What would happen, if when you allowed yourself to go into a new space, you armed yourself with three sets of expectations instead of one, any of which would be possible? Having three expectations instead of one is a psychological attitude to keep your options open. I find it useful to carry my options to their logical conclusion in my fantasy and then if I am still living at the end of them, I can go freely into the new thing. What I have found is that often none of my expectations materialize, but instead other possibilities, which I had not even dreamed of, did. Sometimes the results were spectacular, sometimes dull and boring, and sometimes slightly dangerous, but so far not lethal. The minimum payoff of any of my risk taking is that I have learned something. The biggest was that a whole new and wonderful experience opened before me.

The biggest step that one has to take to open up the new possibilities is namely to take the risk of going into the unknown. The idea of new possibilities can stop with only thinking so the new step stays in a fantasy and never has the chance to become a reality. I've often wondered how many dreams, and how many possibilities have died with their owners without expression.

Preserving the status quo is a way of keeping out a new possibility on the theory that it will make trouble, will shake up the works, so to speak, and create chaos and confusion. Who wants to feel chaotic and be confused? The fact is however that any change requires three phases: First, the honeymoon, the excitement or anxiety phase; second, the phase when things seem all mixed and unfamiliar. How natural, when you stop to think you've never been there before. And third, the integration, when the new part becomes comfortable and familiar to you. Efforts to preserve the status quo (keeping things as they are) are intended to protect one's security, to prevent chaos and confusion, which is thought of only as harmful instead of a normal development of change, since no change can take place without it. Many people have gone to their graves, perhaps prematurely, because they lived on the principle of maintaining the status quo. Staying with the status quo implies there is *only one right way*. When maintaining the status quo is viewed as a choice rather than a must, then new options reveal themselves.

When I was a little girl, I always thought that I must find the one right way which usually meant someone else's, and then spend the rest of my life making it work. I tried to live by the Universal Should List all the time. I also went through a lot of pain and suffering. What I learned was that diapers were a great thing for me up to the age of toilet training, but after that they were ridiculous. I found out that my "one right way" became just as ridiculous after a point. I had to update myself by letting go.

While I was trying to live "one right way" I found I had to act as though I had only "one right face." The rest I had to try to hide some way. It probably was no accident that I was physically sick most of the time until I was forty. What I was really doing was denying the active dynamic process of growth and forcing the energy of my denied parts into eroding my body. We human beings can come out with a lot of ridiculousness and look pretty absurd, especially in retrospect when we have learned better.

Learning new ways is not a matter of being told but one of risking and discovering in a loving, trusting context. People were always telling me how I should be (their way of course). I often used to be accused of being stubborn. Starting out by loving and trusting myself, I found I was willing enough if I were shown new possibilities with love and understanding, and then I could take the steps in my way, taking only those which fit me. The key was in discovering those little steps. I learned I couldn't hurry and there were no shortcuts. I came to "reserve the right to be mentally retarded but educable." Even though I coined that phrase many years ago I increasingly find wisdom in it. It seems that I can learn from my risk taking even though retrospectively it looked foolish.

Looking with new eyes and seeing new possibilities does not mean getting rid of everything in the past that is familiar and comfortable. It means instead a periodic sorting, keeping from the past that which is still effective, letting go that which no longer fits, and adding that which is new and worthy. That which is new finds its place more easily if we acknowledge to ourselves ahead of time that there will most likely be a period of chaos and confusion before it becomes integrated with our other parts. It is like introducing a new in-law into the family—you don't get rid of all the people that were there before. However, many of you have probably been aware of the struggle involved to make a new harmonious relationship a part of the ongoing family.

Many of us have had new doors opened to us because we have been catapulted without warning into a powerful, traumatic situation which required us to cope differently. For some of us that is the only way we have had to make a change. Maybe we don't have to wait for catastrophic things to happen in our lives. Maybe we can have another option as well, by actively and purposefully looking at ourselves and Our Many Faces in a new way. Maybe we can use Our Many Faces to give nourishment, space and opportunity to those other parts of us so they can grow and transform, and make room for the new ones that come along.

Famous Faces

I'd like to play with Our Many Faces in another
way. One of the ways I've found that helps me to
understand things better is to develop a dramatic
context so that I can have fun while I learn. Use
your imagination again and think about famous
people you have known or read about that had a
positive attraction for you, that make you feel
warm and good inside. Choose from people in politics, history, the movies, television, sports, business, religion or any other facet of life, including

fairy tales and the comics. Then think of some people from the same sources who, when you think
about them, repel you. Have at least six altogether,
and write their names down in one column. Then
make another column by writing down the first ad-
jective that comes to your mind when you think
about them. I'll give you an example, using a list of
mine:

Eleanor Roosevelt—	compassionate
Marlene Dietrich—	sexy
King Henry VIII—	selfish
The Old Woman in the Shoe—	overburdened
Aristotle—	wise
Jesus Christ—	loving
Groucho Marx—	funny
Mary, Mary Quite Contrary—	stubborn

When I divide these adjectives into positive and
negative, the positive list comes out compassionate, sexy, wise, loving and funny, all faces I would
be proud to claim to the outside world. The adjectives selfish, overburdened, and stubborn would be
those faces that I would label negative. Formerly,
before I understood what I know now, I would try
to banish all traces of those characteristics I considered negative.

What I have learned is there is a germ of usefulness
in each negative part as well as a germ of destruction in each positive part. For example, there may

be a time when my stubbornness will serve me well as my ability to protect myself and stand my own ground. However, if I use it like a standard procedure every time someone disagrees with me, then I have given it only one use, a destructive one. A further example is my Henry the VIII part; my selfishness may prove extremely beneficial at a time when I am being pressured by other people to do something wrong, or something that doesn't fit me. Then it becomes my self-interest part.

Let me now take a characteristic which I would label positive. My Eleanor Roosevelt part, compassionate, could work to my disadvantage in a situation where instead of being compassionate, I need to be wise. I can thank my Eleanor Roosevelt part for her offer but what I need now is my Aristotle part. Let's take my Marlene Dietrich part, sexy. If I sexualize everything, then I am in the same boat as I was by being stubborn about everything. I know some people who because they got into trouble sexualizing at the wrong time decided that they needed to ban their sexuality altogether. A version of throwing out the baby with the bath water.

Since all of these parts reside in me, then I can say that inside me I have my Eleanor Roosevelt, my Marlene Dietrich, my King Henry VIII, my Old Woman in the Shoe, my Aristotle, my Jesus Christ, my Groucho Marx and my Mary, Mary Quite Contrary.

Let's imagine a meeting of all those people. What will my King Henry VIII say to Eleanor Roosevelt? What will Eleanor Roosevelt say to King Henry? What does Jesus say to Marlene Dietrich, and how does Groucho Marx react to what's going on between Marlene and Jesus? Most of us have had internal dialogues between our various parts, similar to what we saw in the Theater of our Inside. Most of us have experienced an impasse when two parts are in conflict. Perhaps we have also had the feeling that our parts were screaming their heads off and the sound inside was so loud we couldn't hear anything on the outside. These are the times when we make our worst mistakes.

Suppose we think of the negative parts of ourselves as hungry dogs which we want to keep out of our awareness and certainly hide from other people. So we cage them inside (deny their existence) and feed them only when we absolutely have to, and then as little as possible. As they get hungrier and hungrier, we have to increase our guard, for if we let our guard down for even a second, they will come out and make terrible trouble. Continuing in this way we will soon feel exhausted and bankrupt. Despair will soon follow. That is the time when we say we couldn't help it. Someone else made us do it.

The answer is not to get more guards, as many people seem to think, but to start paying attention, caring for and learning to understand these parts. Then instead of using all our energy for guarding (defending) we will be able to use it for discovery and change.

Let's continue the dog story. Suppose we think of the dogs as representing parts of ourselves that have only learned one way of being, and we want to teach them others. Anyone who has ever trained an animal knows they must use love and praise and patience. Would you be willing to be patient and loving and praise yourself? Each dog represents a friend and companion yet undiscovered. To many of us, it looks only like a vicious mongrel. We and our faces are not different from any other living thing. We thrive on being nurtured.

Plants will not grow because you tell them they must, and that they are bad and ugly if they don't. You don't say that if they were intelligent and worthwhile they would do it on their own anyway.

What we do instead with plants is love them, care for them, find out what they need and give them the right sun and water and food, and the plant grows happily. Our parts behave exactly the same way.

Our outside faces are made largely to fit our inside ones and to a great extent our outside faces are determined by the inside ones. Let us go to the Merry-Go-Round in the Amusement Park with this in mind, and watch from the outside the faces that have been made from our insides.

The Merry-Go-Round

A merry-go-round as you know is used mostly by children, but often secretly yearned for by many adults. It has music in the center and around its outsides are a lot of horses going up and down in tune to the music. Let's imagine that there are twelve horses on our merry-go-round and each horse has one of our faces. We are standing and watching it. We will make our merry-go-round go slowly. In this fantasy I am asking you to become an observer of your own faces. Name your faces on the merry-go-round, using the names of the personalities such as Marlene Dietrich and Groucho

Marx, as before, or the case from the Theater of the Inside, such as Anger, Love, Intelligence.

First just watch them as they slowly make the circle. Your eye can pause only for a few seconds on each face because soon another face will come into view. As you see each of these faces, notice how you react to that face. After the merry-go-round has gone around a few times, say clearly to yourself, these are all my faces. Notice which ones you are more familiar with, the ones you especially like, the ones that arouse negative feelings. Now think of each one separately and ask yourself what possible new use or meaning you can find that face. At the same time let yourself know to what use you have been putting each one. As you are doing this, you may become aware that you are missing a face and if you are, add another horse. You may find as you do this you will experience a whole range of feelings, sadness, hope, anger, delight, feelings of well-being and others you may think of that I haven't mentioned. Remember that regardless of the kinds of feelings, they are all yours, and, treated well, Your Many Faces are there to help you.

You may find that one of your faces is in its diaper stage. For example, you may notice your angry face and you will remember you are using it as you did when you were two and you pouted, but now you are thirty-two and you still pout. You know how to pout very well. Could it be that you told yourself that was the only thing to do when you feel angry and therefore that is what you still do? Could you add some other ways of responding, say what you are feeling, give yourself a chance to find out what you are angry about, let yourself know that maybe you are really feeling helpless, and acting angry? Maybe in desperate situations, could you yell? What does it do for you, to let you yourself know you have many choices of using that angry face?

Let's take another example, your face of excitement. When you were twelve and were excited you had to have immediate gratification. Somebody had to listen, right now. Now at twenty-six you are still doing it, thinking it is your personality, and what you have to do. Could you let yourself see the possibility of using that excitement to give yourself a sense of pleasure which you can acknowledge to yourself, that you can invite someone else to share with you, that you can draw a picture, or hum a tune or run a mile?

Let's take a third example; you see your helpless face. When you were eighteen and felt helpless you felt embarrassed or ashamed and you hid. Now at sixty-two or whatever, you still hide. Could you see the possibility of just asking for the help you need? Could you let yourself feel the okayness of feeling helpless because it is human? Or perhaps your helplessness is telling you that you are trying to do something that isn't very constructive. Helplessness often disguises frustration. Once aware of it, you can begin to go in another direction.

Look at all your faces in this manner; think of each one as representing a range of choices. You can't help but add new possibilities to your life as you do this. Can you feel a new sense of your own personal power as you think in this way? You don't have to respond in any one way. You always have possibilities. With this new sense of power it is possible that you can also feel a new sense of responsibility for yourself. What I am suggesting is that when we have choices and can fit the choice to the situation, then we are making choices in front of our face, rather than reacting to compulsions from behind.

There was a time when I thought I had to kill all those parts of me that gave me trouble. Now I see they may be my greatest helpers if I decide to make them my friends.

It does seem backward to go toward the trouble rather than pull away from it. The secret is that when we pull away we only increase the tension and get more and more scared because the trouble doesn't go away. In fact, it seems even bigger and stronger than it actually is. When we go closer we relax the tension. Then we can see the situation for what it really is and make more fitting decisions. Here is an old saying that I just made up. "The more tension you create the blinder and deafer you get and the more stupid and paralyzed you act." It merely means that when you are in a dangerous situation you need all your wits about you. Letting your energy go into maintaining tension draws it from the rest of yourself and freezes your body.

Pressing Your Buttons in Front of Your Face Instead of Allowing Someone to Push Them from Behind

We have talked about choosing rather than acting from compulsion. When you feel that you have to live with someone else's direction or live so that you never disappoint or hurt anybody, then your life is a continual assessment of whether or not you please other people. Then you are having your buttons pushed from behind.

Other people are very much a part of your life. We could not have love and trust relationships if that were not so. However, no matter how much we would like to think differently, we cannot see what goes on inside of another person, even those whom we feel very close to. Furthermore, we are all unique. Therefore, we need to educate other people about ourselves. We do this by sharing what we feel inside (when it fits) with others. It also means that we sometimes need to say no. Of course, someone is bound to be disappointed if we say no.

Disappointment is a perfectly healthy human emotion. To say your "no's" clearly paves the way for honest "yeses." It also lets you be who you are instead of putting up a front.

I am always glad when someone tells me about their inside feelings. I am not as likely then to invade them, nor to hold them responsible for my expectations. I feel on firm ground. It may not always be pleasant, but I know where I stand. I want the same from others, so I am not misunderstood, misinterpreted, or mis-taken. When I am in the process of hiding some of my faces, or have faces that I don't want to accept, then I am in danger of putting on a front. Essentially I give out bum clues. With all my faces fully acknowledged and knowing that I am in charge of me, then I can be in different states at different times and accept that I am capable of error as well as great success. I can then afford to accept me as a person and I can more easily grant you the same possibilities. I can deal with real things rather than my fantasy of them.

Life for me is like an ocean, with waves sometimes high, sometimes low, sometimes smooth, sometimes rough; so sometimes I'm high, sometimes I'm smooth, sometimes I'm low and sometimes I'm troubled. To carry the ocean analogy a little further, the current is life and the waves are essential for the movement of the ocean and for all the life that it holds inside. Waves are a natural response to all of the forces in the universe.

I am the same way, my faces are natural consequences of my being a human being, living and growing, and I need to know that storms as well as the beautiful sunshine are part of life. So I take pride in my stormy face, my sunshiney face, and I accept them as natural for that context. I don't have to put on a happy face when I feel stormy. I can put on a face that belongs with that. And I don't have to put on a face of doubt when I feel sunshiney inside.

In another sense, my faces, my many faces, are all part of my resources with which I respond to my life situation. I have room for thousands in myself. To become acquainted with who lives inside of me, to love and understand my parts, make them grow and assist them to greater harmony with all my other parts is ongoing work. When I see it as human instead of bad I can allow myself to work in the spirit of discovery much like going on an archaeological dig. What will I dig up next? When I know that I am the leader and not the servant, I push my buttons in front of my face instead of feeling pushed from behind.

Which One Is Me?

Did you ever ask yourself that question? Which one is me? Which one of what? When people ask that question, very often they are thinking what is the *real* me? I often hear people say, "Yes, I did that, but that isn't the real me." Me is an expression of myself when I talk, move or act, when I sleep, eat, or do arithmetic problems, when I fantasize, dream and make mistakes, when I'm dirty, clean, or dazzling, when I'm solving great problems or little ones, when I'm helplessly standing by, feeling like nothing or when I'm feeling sexy. When I am choosing and being chosen, so, which one is me? I am all these things.

Actually, I'm coming around to a point I made before, ownership of everything I'm involved in, My Dreams, My Hopes, My Behavior, and My Actions. This is the first step toward managing me. I cannot manage anything I do not own. It might be an interesting thing to make a list of all the many things in which you are involved, and before each subject that you list, write "my." My dream, my hope, my mistake, my angry feeling, and see what it's like for you to recognize your ownership of so many parts. Do it for one day and behold all the reins you have in your hands. Then go through a little ritual and to each one announce very loudly, silently inside yourself, if you are with other people, or out loud if you are alone, "I own you and this is how I would like it to be next time." Since you are the owner and all these parts belong to you, if you would like to make changes, tell your parts and they can only acquiesce to your wishes. Maybe that seems strange that you own everything about yourself. You must be aware after you've done this it could cover a lot of space, a lot of subjects, moods and feelings. You will probably find you have a veritable treasure house in front of you as well as a few bombs. When I do this for myself I have sometimes had a feeling of being overwhelmed. I have also learned that I don't need to do something with everything all at once. I can pick out something I need for now and go to the rest when it fits. They won't go away. But they don't have to be "on my neck," so to speak, because I have a little place with a good storage cabinet. So which one is me? I'm everything that I own. I own everything that I have. Whatever I am using at a moment in time is that "me" expressing itself then. Accepting that with kindness to myself helps me to move on to the next place. I am the only one exactly like me.

I'm the Only One Like Me

I am the only one like me. This could be a frightening thought. Who would your company be if that were totally true? It could also be a comforting thought, in that you are always special. What I am getting at here is that each of us is like everyone else in some very basic ways. Our physiology works pretty much the same and our neurological and sensual systems are also pretty much alike. It is helpful to remind ourselves that we all stem from the same life force. Each of our basic selves is capable of infinite variations. Take the fingerprint for example. Our fingers are capable of doing the same things, they have the same muscles, but every print is unique. It is this uniqueness that gives us our interest in one another. We can count on the fact then that each human being will be different in some way from every other human being.

We all physically have the same ingredients which are capable of functioning in the same way. If we were to see skeletons, we would find variations in length and width of bones, maybe even in the curvature of bones, but we would know that all the joints work in the same way in relation to each other. I am struggling to make clear the relationship between the ingredients themselves, the predictable process of how they operate and the variations of which they are capable. When skin gets near something hot, it will burn. That burn can come from a coal fire, kerosene or an electric stove, and it can come to any skin regardless of color. The burn is caused when vulnerable skin is too close to high heat. The process and the relationship among the parts is what is predictable, all the other aspects are variations. Our differentness lies then in how we think about these relationships, and how much we know about them and how much we are willing to increase their flexibilities.

I would like to compare the words, *variation* and *differentness.* When we see a garden of flowers and notice that there are differences among them, it is easy for us to think of them as *variations.* When we do this we experience good feelings. Variation and variety are thought of as positive. When we see a group of people together and notice that they, like the flowers, are different from each other, we have an inclination to think of these as *differences.* Different somehow brings to mind difficulties and fear, and it is easy to prepare defenses.

Actually, whether it is people or flowers, we are talking about the same thing, how one is the same as or different from the other. If we were to think of people as having variation to each other and then have the good feelings that come with that, we could get our interest and discovery buttons turned on. Witness the allure of travel to countries where people are very different looking and live in exotic ways. I go on the principle that everybody I meet will be different from me in some way which gives me a lot of excitement if I use it that way, and an opportunity to expand myself as I get more experience in incorporating differentness. It might be an interesting thought to think of all disagreements as being the outcome of difference and difference the outcome of variations. Variation is basic to all human beings. We might fight less quickly if we looked at it this way and also we might put more energy into finding more harmonious ways to incorporate the differentness.

There is one area that is constant with each human being, and among human beings, and that is the presence of feeling. All humans feel pain, joy, frustration, anger, calmness, confusion, at some time or another. Each one, however, may not react in the same way to a particular event. What makes one person laugh may make another person cry. What makes one person feel pain might make another person feel excitement. If I take the idea that I am the only one exactly like me seriously then when I meet others, I will go into a discovery process of finding out what parts of that other person are like me and what parts are different from me, instead of making the assumption that because we love each other or are white or black or red or sixty, that we feel and react in the same way. For me that means every person presents an opportunity for me to learn about new variations and it gives me more choices for myself. My Many Faces are my resources to make that possible.

My Many Faces help me to grow and expand and cope successfully with life, but they don't ask me to forget my taste. I don't eat everything on the restaurant menu, marvelous as it may be. I choose the things I like and those not to my taste, I leave. They aren't selected, neither are they rejected. I don't blame them, however, for being there. This is a delicate area sometimes because it is so easy to confuse living by your own preferences with putting other people down. All big supermarkets have a variety of foods. On the whole people select from what there is available, what they want, or what they feel they can afford. They think in terms of what foods will be good for them nutritionally, calorically, and tastewise.

The same thing goes with people. There are some people who we do not feel are nutritious for us. It doesn't mean they are bad, it only means there isn't a fit. Like everything else, one can also develop a taste for things that were previously unknown or distasteful. Sometimes we assume a bad taste too quickly, before we have tried it. And sometimes, having tasted something once, we don't allow ourselves to fully explore before we decide this is not for us. We could cheat ourselves in this way. I see no problem with deciding someone is not to your taste once you have explored in a real way what that is. This is a continuing experience of meeting, exploring and choosing.

Like going into a shoe store, after you have tried on and considered several pairs, you buy the ones that fit. In time they wear out and you get another pair. This is a process of continual selection instead of one of rejection. This time your life situation may have changed, your tastes may have changed and you come out with another pair just as fitting for you now as the other was for you then. It is well to remember that our parts are always changing, and we are in a continual process of sorting, changing, adding, and letting go. That is a part of the miracle. Whatever happens, changes, or stays the same because of this process, I am always the only one exactly like me.

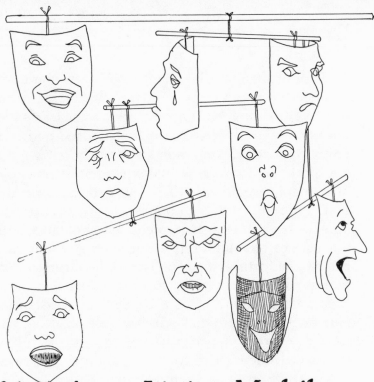

You Are a Living Mobile

Now I would like you to think of yourself, with your many faces, as a living mobile. *Balance* is what makes a mobile work. One can take any number of pieces of different sizes, textures, weights and colors and by placing them in different relation to each other—near, far, sideways, upwards or downwards—one can make a balanced harmonious whole. The mobile is a metaphor for our many parts, balancing, bringing back into balance (rebalancing), being the management of our life. Balance is another word for harmony. When we are out of harmony life seems dark.

Because of the fact that change is always going on and because new things come in, rebalancing is essential from time to time. For example, let's take our physical body. In a perfectly balanced body all parts support themselves in such a way so that no one part has to receive major support from any other part permanently. The legs can stand firmly on the ground, the thigh bones which then can enable the backbone to be straight and in balance and the arms can hang loosely at the sides and the head can be comfortably on top. This is the position our mothers used to want us to have when they said "stand up straight." This is a position of balance. However, if we are stuck with this one position, we can't play, run, dance, walk or any of the other things we humans like to do. As soon as we leave this position, we have to now pay attention to how each part continues to get its support without undermining the rest of the body. What we mean by awkward is that the parts are not in balance. It's perfectly possible to stand on one's head, to stand on only one leg, to be in the air without any ground support at all, as in a ballet leap; however, in order to have this happen, each other part transforms its job so that a balance can take place. Furthermore, no one can stand, for instance, on one leg unless all the other parts are assisting. The search is not for the right form. The search is for the form that fits the task at that moment and a continual rebalancing of all the parts is necessary as the body goes from task to task.

When I was a child and I made a face about something, my mother would say, "Be careful or it will freeze that way." Some of us have sought the right form, tried to live it, and we are frozen. There is no way to write down directions, like a "recipe" for how all bodies are to be in balance. Balance is a feeling of being in touch with one's body, of continually centering energy with the cooperation and conscious support of all the other parts. So we are in the constant process of changing. Change always carries with it a period of imbalance (the scariness and excitement of new possibilities). This happens when something new is being added or something old is going. The feeling of imbalance is often one of confusion. The picture of imbalance can be physical illness, international troubles, competency problems or spiritual desolation. I would go so far as to say that any imbalance is a message about some change taking place. This is a perfectly natural phase because while we are in the process of rebalancing, imbalance has to take place first.

If one views any imbalance in this way, then one goes on with the rebalancing and the process of that is to listen for the message of the imbalance, find out what it's about. There will probably be some trial and error attempts, trying out some new knowledge and awareness. If on the other hand the state of imbalance, the natural result of change, is looked upon as a comment on danger of failure, then fear will take over. Here's where paralysis, deafness, dumbness and huge mistakes get made. Balance is another way of talking about harmony. Every individual has beliefs about how he or she should be. There come times in every individual's life where what they want is different from what they think they ought to do and that is different from what they think they can do. This is a typical out-of-balance situation. This is a position of pain.

Many people attempt to balance this type of an imbalance by going to the rules about how they should be and commit themselves to putting up with pain instead of looking at the literal position they are in in that particular situation. When these all come together at the same time, the person faces a balance problem.

Having periods of imbalance is a natural consequence of living. To stay in an imbalanced state will make for great erosion and pain to the self. It is always scary when we are out of balance, because it feels like we have lost our center. A very important thing to do at that point is to sit in the nearest chair, close your eyes and breathe fully. Then tell yourself, "I am getting a message that my parts are out of harmony. I am getting an S.O.S message." Then start listening to what your parts are telling you. Look at what is happening, find out what the needs seem to be, and then search to find out what to do about it.

For instance you might be having a headache. Treat the headache first, as a big signal that something is out of balance, jammed together, or in some way being underfed or unnoticed. Maybe you're hungry and your stomach is telling you it has been without food for too long. Maybe your digestive system is stopped up. Maybe you have been cramping some nerves that are cutting off circulation of blood to your brain. Maybe you have been breathing shallowly and haven't enough oxygen, maybe you have caught yourself in the middle of a dilemma which pulls on either side, which causes your brain to be paralyzed. Maybe you're sustaining an awful lot of anger which you haven't acknowledged. In this case, some things come from your body, some come from your feelings, some from your thoughts. Any and all of them could be operating to give you a headache. There is a tendency to think in terms of one thing alone. The chances are there are many parts operating. If my stomach is clamoring for food and there has been no food intake because I have been busy feeling depressed, and I am feeling depressed because I feel like a failure and I feel like a failure because somebody left me, my headache is really the outcome of all these things working together.

It is important to realize that if you would decide that you should just feed your stomach no matter what, the headache could persist, although your hungry stomach is part of it. You could have thought your depression was a natural outcome of your having some terrible experience. Because you thought that the depression was a natural outcome you wouldn't see it as having any relationship to your headache. What is so often the usual effort on the part of the human mind is to find one cause and think that if that gets fixed all the other things will be fixed. This would be a panacea. It goes even further than that if I happen to fix my headache by eating poached eggs, it would be an easy thing to think that eating poached eggs will cure headaches. People are often disappointed that their panacea doesn't work.

When something goes wrong I try to make a picture in my mind of a circle with myself in the center and then ask myself what part in my problem are my thoughts playing, my fears, my nutrition, my exercise, my expectations, my interpretations, what people are telling me from the outside, what the weather is like and my faith in being able to grow. I could easily have questions about what people are telling me, or my faith—or have I eaten junk food—have I been too sedentary—have I been taken in by something from the outside—all of which have upset my balance and caused the signal which made me feel uncomfortable. We human beings seem to need being hit over the head by a loud message like a terrible physical pain or a big upset with somebody we care about or a huge loss to know that we are out of balance.

From time to time things go wrong with any good piece of machinery. Yet most machines have built into them some way of signaling when things aren't working right or are out of balance or harmony.

This is usually a red light. We have the same signal system built in; the minute we see the red light on the machine we stop and take a look. Our signals come on when we feel out of balance and I am recommending we take a look.

Once we have seen our red signal and interpreted it as something out of balance in ourselves, we may, if we listen and look carefully, find a clue as to how to change it. However, after much search, we may find that we can't find a clue. So the sensible thing then is to find someone who can go on the search with us, a family member, a friend, a teacher, a spiritual counselor or some professional person from the healing arts. The important thing here is to find someone who will discover *with* you, together, instead of telling you how you ought to be.

It is important also to acknowledge what we might consider little imbalances and then we can deal with them before they become big imbalances. Now let's just ask ourselves, is it okay to want things? Is it okay to have shoulds which are usually ideas about duty and responsibility? and then awarenesses about one's capacity at a moment in time? For example, is it possible to be physically tired and need to sleep, want to go to a dance, and feel that you should stay home and do your homework? If you have a *rule* that you should always do the right thing, then you have to settle for your duty whether you are tired or whether you want something else or not. If your *rule* is that life is

made for doing everything you want to do regardless of your fatigue level, or your other responsibilities, then chances are pretty good that you will still
be out of balance because you will feel guilty. If
you believe that you can only do what you can do,
never mind your responsibilities or what you want,
you are still in the same boat, really. Your mobile
has no chance for any flexibility. Every time the
wind blows, it will break. What would happen if
instead of having a *rule* that covers all situations all
the time, you were able to pick and *choose* within
the situation? That is, sometimes you will choose
for duty, sometimes to suit your wishes and sometimes what you feel you can do. All of these parts
are capable of stretching and if you know yourself,
you have a guide that permits you to make the best
choice in relation to each given situation. Then you
will not suffer the pain of the "cookie cutter."
Cookie cutter is a term I use to mean forcing the
same thing for all times and in all situations. It cuts
off some of your important parts, and that is painful.

Students of life find out that there is such a thing as
winning a battle and losing a war as for every gain
there is a loss, and conversely for every loss there is
a gain; so therefore in one funny sense each decision is a new creation with a new set of losses and
gains. In other words, you are balancing out your
needs with your responsibilities with your wishes,
by making that decision fresh each time.

Sometimes we can take one loss and sometimes we can take another. Each situation presents a different equation of loss and gain. If we are free to vary our approaches we can continue to create new balance and keep up to date with ourselves.

Making Your Own Road Map

The beginning of new possibilities starts when you have a deep bone-like conviction that there are no fixed permanent sets of roadways in your insides, that they are all capable of being resurfaced, re-shaped, reconstructed, bypassed and built anew. We come into this planet at birth and leave at death. The time between these two points is our time in which we develop our own map. It will continue to unfold, if you allow yourself to explore your many parts and risk going into the unknown. Some people make up a detailed map at five and then spend their lives fitting into it. Others start out with a large space and proceed to follow the continual process of discovery which shifts and changes the points on our map and the lines between them as we move, look, listen, speak, sort, challenge, take in and let go.

Our first map is usually made up of the one right way, a set of shoulds and a fixed goal, judged by the yardstick of good, bad, right and wrong. At that time perhaps this is essential because we have not yet developed our resources. For it to be used as a way of life it means then that only a few of our parts can have life because the others are kept in hiding. Even the accepted faces of ourselves cannot live fully because the hidden parts are draining off our vital energy. We have much more literal knowledge available to us than what most of us realize or that is coming to the mainstream of attitudes about human beings. Did you know that each of your cells has its own separate intelligence? Did you know that all life is made up of cells? And that each cell has the program for the totality of our body and maybe the universe? Did you know that your thoughts have an effect on whether your cells grow freely or with obstruction? Our cells cannot release their intelligence when our brain is rendering them either unintelligible or asking them to go in an opposite direction.

Today is an exciting time, because almost every day some new information about life's processes is coming to light. Maybe one of the kindest things we can do for ourselves at this moment is to take a look at everything we believe in and ask ourselves if it really fits or is it something that we were told should fit. Is it a carryover from the past that we have accepted without any critical investigation?

We have now come to the end of the adventure I promised you. If it stimulated you to new possibilities, and provided you with new ideas and information, you can now continue on your own special journey. You have one life, only one, and it is yours. You are the architect. Each architect works with slightly different materials and you, the only one exactly like you in the whole world, are your own material.

I find it useful to give myself a focus by writing things down. I suggest you start by writing down a list of new things that you would like—new attitudes with which you would like to experiment; new aspects of yourself that you would like to learn more about. Then write down three things you could do to further each of these, such as read a book, talk to someone, meditate, join a group, or attend a seminar or lecture. Having *three* approaches helps to keep from getting embroiled in an either/or situation. If you like to fantasize or visualize, do so; it will provide additional energy while you write down your approaches.

While writing this list, it is possible that new ideas

may continue to occur to you because you are probably in a creative frame of mind. If so, treat them as new possibilities to consider along with the rest. Explorers have a goal, but they also take time to see other possibilities along the way, which may change their course.

After making the list, and writing down your three approaches, give yourself a clear message to start with one of them and put it into action. I find it useful to keep a journal, written in as detailed or as general a way as I have time for, to keep track of what happens as I venture into new territory.

Something else that I find helpful is to gather together all the pictures I have of myself so that I can see myself in my many different moods, activities, and stages of life, and accept them all as belonging to me. I encourage people to make what I call My Book of Me, which contains these pictures as well as pictures of people I care about. I include excerpts from the journal, writing of new things I have attempted; different ways I have coped with the same situation over time; reports of dreams, night and day; and whatever other bits of things that are part of my experience, so that I can get a sense of my own continuity as I journey through life.

Everyone, no matter what age, has new things to discover about themselves. To the degree that we discover these things, we become more interesting people to ourselves and to others. To the degree that we accept ourselves in all our parts, we become whole, loving beings in relation to ourselves, which helps us to become more real and loving to other people. Our struggles become creative ventures, not always without pain, but with the hope of more effective results.

So bon voyage to you as you continue your journey, discovering and rediscovering the miracle that is you. I send you and myself loving and caring messages to encourage the taking of new risks. One day we may meet again.

AHP Journal, Association for Humanistic Psychology, 325 Ninth St., San Francisco, CA 94103

Assagioli, Roberto. *The Act of Will.* New York: Viking Press, 1973

Branden, Nathaniel. *Breaking Free.* New York: Bantam Books, 1972.

_____ *Psychology of Self-Esteem.* New York: Bantam Books, 1971.

Green, Elmer & Green, Alyce. *Beyond Biofeedback.* New York: Delacorte Press, 1977.

Huxley, Laura Archera. *Between Heaven and Earth: Recipes for Living & Loving.* New York: Farrar, Straus & Giroux, 1975.

_____ *You Are Not the Target.* New York: Farrar, Straus & Giroux, 1963.

Missildine, W. Hugh. *Your Inner Child of the Past.* New York: Simon & Schuster.

Montague, Ashley. *Touching: The Human Significance of the Skin.* New York: Columbia University Press, 1971.

Ott, John N. *Health & Light.* Old Greenwich: Devin-Adair, 1973.

Progroff, Ira. *At a Journal Workshop: The Basic Text & Guide for Using the Intensive Journal.* Dialogue House, 1975.

_____ *Peoplemaking*. Palo Alto, CA: Science & Behavior Books, 1972.

Schwarz, Jack. *The Path of Action.* New York: Dutton, 1977.

Selye, Hans. *Stress Without Distress.* New York: Lippincott. 1974.

Shealy, C. Norman, M.D. *Ninety Days to Self-Health.* New York: Dial Press, 1977.

Skutch, Judith, Publisher. *A Course in Miracles,* Foundation for Inner Peace, 1 West 81st St., Suite 5D, New York, NY 10024.

Synthesis, a journal devoted to further integration of the person, 830 Woodside Road, Redwood City, CA 94061.

ABOUT THE AUTHOR

Described by Human Behavior magazine as "Everybody's Family Therapist," Virginia Satir has spent her life peeking at, looking under, and poking into what goes on between and among human beings. Her formal search began forty years ago when she started her professional life teaching handicapped and gifted children, which led her to looking at their families for psychological, social, and therapeutic clues.

Virginia Satir's philosophy is that the human being is a miracle, always evolving and capable of continued growth and change and new understanding. Her focus is on what makes people nurturing, happy, and effective, as well as understanding what makes them sick, troubled and ineffective.

She has been increasingly interested in bringing the rich and useful concepts from human psychology to the general public in direct and clear ways. Her books, films, and videotapes are presented from that point of view. She is the author of *Conjoint Family Therapy*

118

(1964), now published in eight languages and often referred to as the "Bible" for family therapists; *Peoplemaking* (1972), a popular book also published in eight languages, which uses a family context to focus on the experiences and processes which go into our becoming persons; and *Self Esteem* (1974) and *Making Contact* (1976), two other popular books. She also collaborated with John Grinder and Richard Bandler in a book called *Changing With Families* (1976), and has published various articles and chapters in professional journals and anthologies.

Virginia was educated at the University of Wisconsin and the University of Chicago. She holds an honorary doctorate from the University of Wisconsin, and was recently awarded the gold medal for "outstanding and consistent service to mankind" by the University of Chicago.

At the present time, Virginia Satir carries on training in what she calls human communication and human systems, which now include large business and governmental systems in eleven countries. She is a "roving professor" at many universities on the North American continent, and is a consultant to numerous social and health agencies.

BOOKS OF RELATED INTEREST

HOW TO BE SOMEBODY by noted psychologist Yetta Bernhard presents a specific guide for personal growth that will "lead to acceptance of one's self as a human being." 96 pages, soft cover, $3.95.

SELF-CARE by Yetta Bernhard explains to the reader the importance of saying "I count," and describes exactly how to put the premise of self-care into practical everyday living. 228 pages, soft cover, $6.95.

MAKING CONTACT by Virginia Satir shows how you can better understand the basic tools for making contact with others and explains how you can use them to work for change in your perceptions, your actions, and your life. 96 pages, soft cover, $3.95.

SELF ESTEEM by Virginia Satir is a simple and succinct declaration of self-worth for the individual in modern society looking for new hope, new possibilities, and new, positive feelings about themselves. 64 pages, soft cover, $3.50.

POSITIVE SELFISHNESS: A Practical Guide to Self-Esteem by Frieda Porat with Margery Quackenbush addresses the central problem in the search for personal fulfillment. Dr. Porat presents techniques which illustrate the dynamics and purpose of a healthy love of self. 180 pages, soft cover, $4.95.

SELECTIVE AWARENESS by Peter H.C. Mutke, M.D., offers you an opportunity to break through to a new level of health and vigor using the amazing new technique that gives you control of the healing and growth potential within you. 204 pages, soft cover, $4.95.

Available at your local book or department store or directly from the publisher. To order by mail, send check or money order to:

Celestial Arts
231 Adrian Road
Millbrae, CA 94030

Please include $1.00 for postage and handling. California residents add 6% tax.